MARCONI'S
BATTLE FOR RADIO

Beverley Birch
Illustrated by Robin Bell Corfield

VICTOR GOLLANCZ
LONDON

At the ship's rail the three men hunched deep in their heavy winter coats. Icy winds blasted from the open sea, and they had to squint through sea spray as the ship nosed into the narrow neck of water towards the harbour.

At once they saw the great cliff. From its snowy rock, a tower gazed ahead to the harbour and back across the wilderness of the Atlantic Ocean where icebergs drifted like vast white mountains.

Was this the place where they could make their dream come true?

They did not ask the question aloud. Not a single person on that ship knew why they had sailed from England ten days ago, why they had crossed 3200 kilometres of freezing winter seas to reach this distant corner of Newfoundland.

It was a secret, and they must keep it so.

The problem was that these three men were famous. People liked reading about them; at the slightest excuse reporters would take ship and train to track them down.

The three men weren't ready for that. Not yet.

And so they waited for the ship to dock, huddled in their greatcoats, impatient to step ashore. First went Marconi, and then his two assistants, Kemp and Paget; and behind them a strange assortment of luggage hauled from the ship's hold and piled on the quayside.

Wooden crate after wooden crate ... a huge
hamper big enough to take a large animal,
but light for its size ... long metal cylinders ...

Across the ocean, on a far-away tip of
England, a group of specially-chosen people
also waited, also impatient, to hear that
Marconi and his team had landed.

First, they must find the right place to work. Somewhere high. Somewhere with a view straight across the ocean towards England.

Somewhere like that hill by the harbour channel.

They all had a good look at it, particularly Kemp – for Kemp would have to launch the balloons and kites packed in that large hamper. He trudged round, plodding through drifting snow. Was there room enough to anchor ropes for holding kites against this roaring wind?

Marconi and Paget hurried in and out of the old buildings. A splendid shelter for their equipment!

It was Friday 6 December 1901 when they climbed that hill. It was bitterly cold and getting colder, and all the time they fought the fear that the vicious weather would never let them do what they had come to do.

We know their thoughts because they wrote diaries of this day and the days that followed, and you can still read them now, more than 90 years later, and see how each of them felt.

Soon that hill-top echoed to the chop of pick-axes, as local men hacked at the frozen earth and heaved plates of metal about. Marconi, Kemp and Paget raced to get their equipment safe and dry under shelter.

As they worked away on that icy hill, the twentieth century (our century) was not yet two years old. It was 1901. There was no television or radio. Using electricity at all – for lights or machines – was very new.

But people had learned to send a message
by electricity – as long as a wire carrying the
electricity joined the sender to the receiver.

No wire – no message.

That is, not until Marconi came along.

That was why Marconi was already famous. To the watching world he had conjured a kind of magic in the air above the earth. He had sent messages vibrating *through the air without wires.* No physical link joined sender to receiver; and Marconi's messages winged their way at the speed of light – 300,000 kilometres each second!

Scientists had said it was not possible. They knew all about the mysterious, invisible electrical waves, and to think of sending them more than a few kilometres was just a dream!

It wasn't. Marconi had done it. He had sent the electrical vibrations into the air, as far as he wanted. He had caught them back from the air, just as he chose.

That was six years before, at home in Italy.
He'd only sent them from one end of an attic
room to the other, watched by his mother ...

But months followed, while he fiddled with bits of wire and metal. He struggled to make the vibrations jump longer distances between the equipment that sent them, the *transmitter*, and the equipment that caught them, the *receiver*.

His brother Alfonso became his constant helper, guarding the receiver, raising a shout of glee each time the surge of electricity sent by Marconi from the attic set the receiver's buzzer tingling.

First, Alfonso carried it down from floor to floor of the great house. Then out on to the sunny terrace. Then, armed with a white flag to wave when the buzzer sounded, he strode away through fields and orchards ...

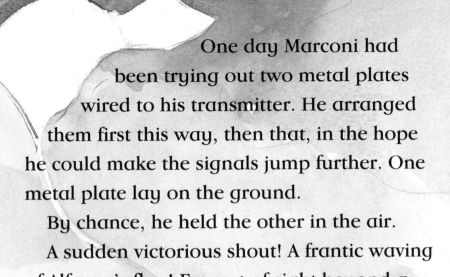

One day Marconi had
been trying out two metal plates
wired to his transmitter. He arranged
them first this way, then that, in the hope
he could make the signals jump further. One
metal plate lay on the ground.

By chance, he held the other in the air.

A sudden victorious shout! A frantic waving
of Alfonso's flag! Far out of sight beyond a
ridge, the buzzer had buzzed.

The vibrations had flown across hills!

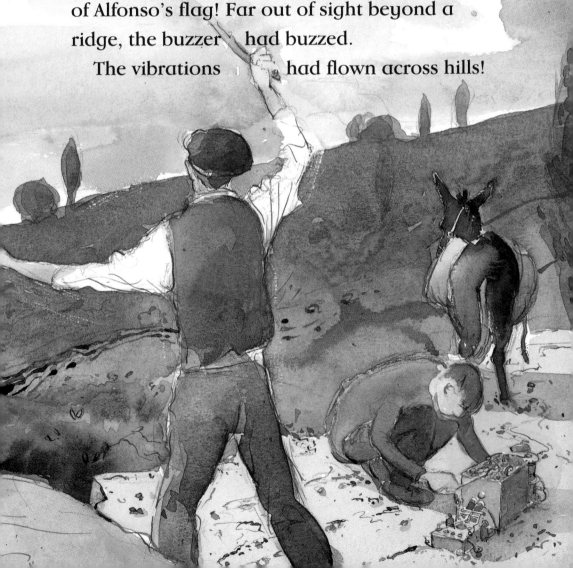

A vast jump – just because of a metal plate held high in the air! Over the next six years Marconi worked and worked to get the arrangement right. He changed the air plate for a copper wire and called it an *aerial*. The ground plate was the *earth*.

Week by week, month by month, he sent the electrical vibrations (now called *radio waves*) over longer stretches of land and water. By 1901 they could travel 360 kilometres.

Now Marconi faced the challenge of the Atlantic: 3200 kilometres of unbroken water.

Again scientists said he could not succeed. They believed that radio waves moved in straight lines. The earth was curved, so (they said) radio waves travelling any distance would shoot out into space. The earth's curve between America and England made the bulge of the ocean like a water-mountain 240 kilometres high!

But secretly Marconi prepared: first, a new radio station at Poldhu on the south-west coast of England, with a towering ring of poles to carry the aerials high into the air ...

Next he explored a map of the world, tracing a line from the coast of England westwards, across the Atlantic Ocean. He found the east coast of America, and searched for the best place to build a second radio station. There must be nothing but unbroken sea between the two.

Cape Cod. There, on the hook of land jutting out into the sea. Marconi and his team crossed the ocean and set to work. Slowly the new radio station rose into the air – a ring of gigantic masts, just like Poldhu.

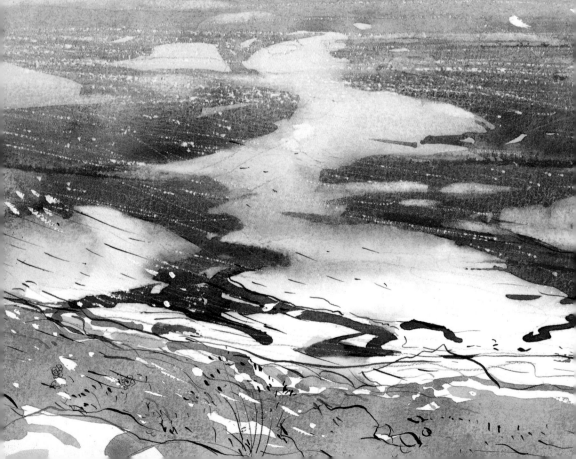

Then, disaster! Vicious winds tumbled the masts at Poldhu like match-sticks. The Poldhu men drew deep breaths, and began again ...

But then gales roared through the aerials at Cape Cod and left a heap of broken wood and tangled wires.

So Marconi came to the snow-swept hill named Signal Hill, bringing kites and balloons. His two grand Atlantic stations were in ruins, but it would not stop his dream.

Signal Hill, Newfoundland, also faced straight across the sea to England.

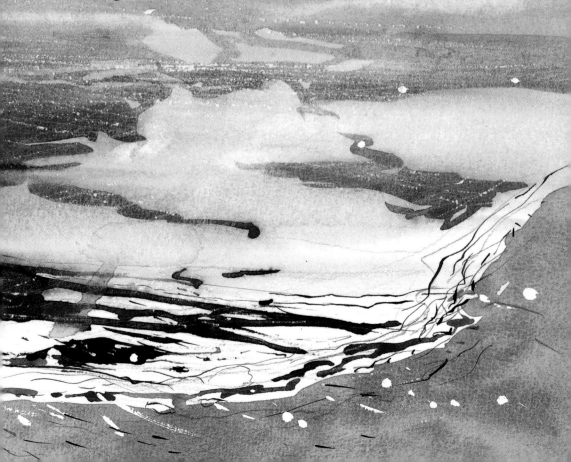

In England the team had rebuilt Poldhu, with lower masts to carry the aerials. These would send out the radio waves.

On Signal Hill, Marconi, Kemp and Paget would try to catch them with aerials flown in the air on the balloon.

And now they were setting out the delicate equipment Marconi would use. The device to show whether radio waves had crossed the ocean was tiny – a narrow glass tube, no bigger than a thermometer. Inside were finely-ground filings of different metals.

Usually the filings rested loosely in the tube. But if electricity reached them, they clung together or 'cohered', giving the device its name – a *coherer*. There was also a little tapper attached – a tiny piece of metal to knock the tube and shake the metal filings loose again.

The coherer was linked to the aerial. When an electrical vibration touched the aerial, a burst of electricity ran down the wire to the filings in the tube. These would stick together and let the electricity pass across them – they formed a *switch*, switching electricity 'on'. At once the tapper would knock the filings loose and the electricity would switch 'off' again.

But when no vibrations reached the aerial the metal filings remained loose and the electricity stayed 'off'.

Usually Marconi connected the coherer to a Morse-code machine. This tapped out short and long bursts of electricity as short and long sounds to show letters of the alphabet, or punched them as dots and dashes on paper. But at Signal Hill he worried that radio waves travelling all the way from Poldhu might arrive too weak to work the Morse machines.

Instead, he connected a telephone earpiece to the coherer: his ear might hear a click as each electrical pulse arrived and the metal filings clung together.

Trails of wire linked everything together, and led outside.

From there, Kemp would fasten one wire to a flying kite or balloon to form the aerial. Another wire linked the coherer to the metal plates which the local men had buried in the ground outside – these were the earths.

Through Sunday they worked on, testing, adjusting, testing again.

Monday came and went. The weather grew darker and fiercer.

Tuesday dawned. It was wet and foggy. But to their delight the winds were milder – calm enough to risk launching a kite. It swooped and twisted, and Kemp ran to and fro – a guide-rope loosened here, tightened there ...

One whipped free and they rushed to trap and anchor it. A sudden slackening of the rope as the kite fell, then too sharp a wind-tug, and a thick rope might snap like thin cotton thread!

The ropes held, and they had the kite safely in the air.

It was time to tell Poldhu.

They went down to the town and sent the message to England on the cable telegraph that lay along the bed of the Atlantic. Each day, for three continuous hours, over and over again, Poldhu must send out the same radio signal – the letter 'S' in Morse code: three short dots. On Signal Hill they would try to catch it.

Wednesday roared in with storms – but they refused to let the weather stop them now.

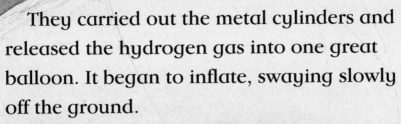

They carried out the metal cylinders and released the hydrogen gas into one great balloon. It began to inflate, swaying slowly off the ground.

Kemp wrestled with the guide-ropes. The winds tugged at them, frantic, and the balloon tossed into the air, juddering.

Marconi lifted the earphone. Storm electricity crackled and hissed. The wind howled and the cliff thundered to the angry rhythm of the sea. How could he hear radio signals in all this?

Across the ocean in Poldhu the Morse-code operator pressed a long lever – tap, tap, tap. At each press, electricity jumped between two metal balls with a crash and a blinding blue spark. Out along the aerial wires travelled the vibrations, away and over the wintery sea.

Could Marconi – 3200 kilometres away – possibly catch that signal a moment later?

On Signal Hill the balloon snapped at the ropes, watched anxiously by Kemp. Nothing in Marconi's ear but storm and wind.

12 o'clock came and went. 1 o'clock. 2 o'clock ...

Click click click!

Or was it?

Outside, Kemp used all his strength to tighten the ropes and hold the swaying monster balloon steady. If the aerials ripped off, they would have to start all over again.

Crack! The ropes snapped and the balloon shot into the air, lost among the clouds.

Now it was too dark and they were too exhausted to go on.

Thursday broke colder and greyer, with lashing rain. They decided to try a kite this time. They had six. If they lost these, they would lose the battle.

The first kite wheeled and swooped like a wild bird frantic to get free, and they fought to stop it plunging against the cliff.

Paget was outside now. Kemp and Marconi took turns at the earphone ...

Snap! The wind won. The kite whipped up and vanished in the mists.

Out came the second kite, and up into the air, nearly taking Kemp with it.

Marconi bent over the table, straining to hear. As the gale tossed the kite like a feather, the aerial kept changing height above the land and so changing its chance of catching any signals. It could never work in these miserable conditions!

Minutes ticked by. Not a single click in the earphone.

Was there something wrong with the instruments? Something wrong at Poldhu? How would they *know* if the problem was at Poldhu?

Paget hauled at the twisting kite, desperate to hold it steady at one height. The wind flung it away from him, higher ...

A sudden click in Marconi's ear. He crouched over the earphone. The tapper striking the coherer! Electricity spurting down from the aerial!

Something was coming.

Three sharp clicks – close to each other. Unmistakable. The three dots of the Morse 'S'! From Poldhu.

Silence.

He passed the earphone to Kemp. Kemp
listened. Nothing. Only the crackle of
the storm.

Click click click. Kemp *did* hear them!

They called Paget, but Paget was a bit
deaf and heard nothing.

They listened again.

The kite soared upwards and suddenly it
was the right height to catch the waves. Three
clicks in the earphone, then three more …
S-S-S-S … a whole train of them!

But still they kept the secret from the
world. Just one more try. Just to be sure!

Hailstones and hurricane winds fought
them the next day. Yet through it all came the
dots – faint, fading as the kite circled, but
always coming again, reaching them over
and over.

Now they could let the secret out.

They told the newspapers on Saturday,
eight days after landing on Newfoundland.
In no more than the twinkling of an eye, radio
signals had winged across the world!

And so these days of struggle against
Atlantic gales have gone down as one of those
great landmarks in our history.

There were many years of difficult work
ahead before they could give us the kind of
radio we have now – with voices or music from
anywhere in the world at the push of a button
or the turn of a knob.

But those were the beginnings – those icy
days on Signal Hill when Marconi, Kemp
and Paget plucked the first 'S' from the air –
and proved to the world that it could be done.

The rest is another story ...

Today, we can get information and entertainment by radio from anywhere in the world, straight into our homes. We can call for help across vast distances. Radio is a lifeline for anyone at sea, or in the air, or in any place where there are no wires to link them by electricity or telephone to the rest of us. Even the depths of the ocean and outer space can now be reached.

Before the beginning of the story in this book, there were many years of work on radio by many people in different places. And after Marconi's triumph, there were still years of work ahead, to give us the sort of radio we now have.

It took Marconi and his team another year of work in Canada before they could successfully send signals back across the Atlantic Ocean, from Nova Scotia to England. They did not really know how radio waves travelled, and it was not for another twenty years, in the 1920s, that they found out enough to control the radio waves properly.

Then Marconi and other scientists had to learn
how to control the lengths of the radio waves
(called the wave-lengths). They had to develop
better equipment for sending
the radio waves (the
transmitters) and better
equipment for receiving the
waves (the detectors and
receivers) too.

A much better detector than Marconi's coherer
was invented, called a thermionic valve.
Eventually, this development meant that spoken
words and music could be transmitted, and not
just Morse Code. Radio programmes to entertain
people began to be broadcast in the 1920s.
And all the time, work continued on sending
radio signals over longer distances. Short
wave radio was developed, and in
1948 the transistor radio was
invented. That was the
beginning of the kind of
radio we enjoy and use
now.

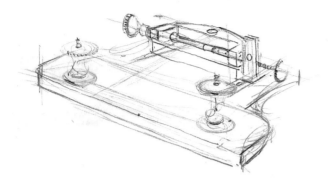

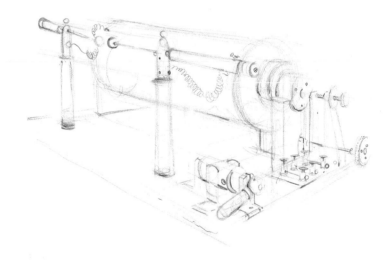

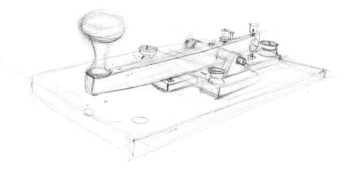